THE JUDGMENT SEAT OF CHRIST

Daniel Kolenda

With

Dr. Robert Gladstone

CfaN CHRIST FOR ALL NATIONS

Australia • Brazil • Canada • Germany • Hong Kong • Singapore
South Africa • United Kingdom • United States

The Judgment Seat of Christ, *The Lost Treasure Series*
By Daniel Kolenda
© 2016, Christ for all Nations

Published by Christ for all Nations (USA)
PO Box 590588
Orlando, FL 32859-0588
www.CfaN.org

The Judgment Seat of Christ Paperback   978-1-933446-40-0
The Judgment Seat of Christ EBOOK   978-1-933446-41-7
El Tribunal de Cristo Paperback - Spanish 978-1-933446-42-4
El Tribunal de Cristo EBOOK - Spanish   978-1-933446-43-1

Editorial: Sheila Chase Greco & Marian Belmonte
Interior Design: by Grupo Nivel Uno Inc.
Cover Design: Designs2Go

First Edition – 1st printing

Printed in Colombia

SPECIAL THANKS TO:

Pastors Garry and Kim Wiggins, Evangel Temple Assembly of God, Jacksonville, Florida – where this book was born.

Harvey and Howard Katz. It was on our fishing trip in B.C. that this theme was stirred in my heart afresh. Many of the thoughts from our rich conversation influenced the content of this material.

H AVE YOU EVER PLAYED A WORD ASSOCIATION game? Word association is an interesting way to see how someone categorizes and connects ideas, feelings, experiences, and information. So if I say a word, what is the first thought that comes to your mind? For instance, if I say "dog" you might think "cat." If I say "heart" you may think "love." If I say "fur" you might think "coat."

But what if I said "judgment"?

What comes to your mind? Almost certainly you would associate negative thoughts with judgment. In fact, our modern world hates few ideas more than judgment. The one Bible verse that most unbelievers seem to know is, "Judge not so you will not be judged" (Matt. 7:1). Even many Christians now ignore—or even reject—the idea of judgment altogether.

It is true that human judgments are flawed at best and corrupt at worst. And there is nothing more repulsive than chronic criticism and judgmentalism. But when it comes to God's judgments, they are as wonderful and perfect as He is. That means we should not avoid the

Judge not so you will not be judged, NKJV

theme of God's judgments. Rather, as true followers of His Son, we should understand and appreciate them.

One of the reasons for confusion around this topic is that, for many people, the subject of God's judgment seems to contradict other doctrines they hold dear. For example, didn't Jesus say, "Whoever hears my word and believes him who sent me has eternal life. He *does not come into judgment*, but has passed from death to life" (John 5:24)? And yet Paul says explicitly, "We must all appear before the judgment seat of Christ" (2 Cor. 5:10). Both statements are true without any contradictions because they are not referring to the same event, but to different judgments. In fact, Scripture describes a number of distinct judgments—past, present, and future.

> Whoever hears my word and believes him who sent me has eternal life. He does not come into judgment, but has passed from death to life, NIV

Even though Christians are exempt from the final judgment by the blood of Jesus, it is important for us to consider God's judgments for two reasons. First, they reveal the profound mystery of His character. David declares, "Your judgments are like a great deep" (Ps. 36:6). They display the unfathomable fusion of righteousness and mercy in God's nature. "He will judge the world in righteousness and will execute judgment for the peoples with equity" (Ps. 9:8). Yet in the very next verse, "The Lord also will be a stronghold for the oppressed, a stronghold in times of trouble" (Ps. 9:9).

That is why, even in the New Testament, God's judgments are actually celebrated. They are not relics of the past, belonging exclusively to the Old Testament. They reveal His glory even under the New Covenant. Remember that Jesus said the Father has "given all judgment to the Son" (John 5:22) and "in righteousness [Jesus the King] judges and wages war" (Rev. 19:11). Our Lord and Savior Jesus Christ, the One who died on the cross and whose blood was shed for the salvation of the world, is now the great Judge, and the Father has given all judgment into His hand. Since all judgment now and in the future is the domain of Christ, there could be nothing more "New Covenant" than this theme. I realize that this contradicts the easy-go-lucky, hippy flower child version of Jesus that so many modern Christians believe in. But the Scriptural Jesus (the only true Jesus) is quite different than most people understand. Listen to how John describes Him in Revelation.

"His head and His hair were white like white wool, like snow; and His eyes were like a flame of fire. His feet *were* like burnished bronze, when it has been made to glow in a furnace, and His voice *was* like the sound of many waters. In His right hand He held seven stars, and out of His mouth came a sharp two-edged sword; and His face was like the sun shining in its strength. When I saw Him, I fell at His feet like a dead man..." (Revelation 1:14-17)

This is the Jesus that is sitting at the right hand of God—the Judge and King of all the earth. The theme of God's judgment spans the length of human history, and is as marvelous as it is sober. It is both awesome and frightening, wonderful and terrible, just and merciful.

Second, Christians should consider God's judgments because, in one way or another, it is a subject that directly affects all of us. We will all in fact stand before "the judgment seat of Christ" in order to have our works evaluated as we enter the glory of the age to come. Yes, we are justified by faith and should have no fear of damnation. But we should be very sobered by the fact that the burning eyes of Christ will analyze our "deeds done in the body" to see if they are fit to follow us into His eternal Kingdom. This theme is not at all popular today, but that does not mean it is not true. As you will see, it is very important and merits earnest consideration.

"Since you call on a Father who judges each person's work impartially, live out your time as foreigners here in reverent fear." (1 Pet. 1:17, NIV). As followers of Jesus, we are wise to reflect on the severity of God's justice while celebrating the sweetness of His mercy. So let's take a step back and consider some of God's awesome judgments throughout biblical history. Then we will focus on the judgment that applies to us as believers: the judgment seat of Christ. This will help us to live with joyful anticipation, as well as careful sobriety, as we journey toward eternity.

The Judgment of Adam and Eve in the Garden of Eden (GEN. 3:14–24)

THE STORY IS WELL KNOWN. SO WELL KNOWN, IN FACT, that it's easy to miss its force through sheer familiarity. But this account of original sin and God's first judgment is no literary invention or Sunday school cliché. It is a compelling sketch of justice and mercy. Images of a new world, God's lovely Garden, Adam and Eve, that ol' crafty serpent, and the forbidden fruit actually lay out a powerful narrative that establishes three foundational truths on which God's future judgments—including His work of salvation—will rest.

First, God respects human choices. The same free will that is our greatest dignity can potentially be our greatest downfall as it was in the Garden.

Second, God's judgment on Adam and Eve declares that He is just. "Righteous are You, O Lord, and upright are Your judgments" (Ps. 119:137)! God is good and upright to the core. Justice and equity naturally, eternally, and incandescently permeate His entire being. So it is impossible for Him to overlook human sins. He simply cannot deny Himself. He must act consistently with His own just nature.

Thirdly, God's judgment on Adam and Eve, however, also reveals His mercy. God is a good Father, and will always work for His children's ultimate good. Yes, He is committed to teaching righteousness to His children, and will use judgments to do that when necessary: "For when the earth experiences Your judgments, the inhabitants of the world learn righteousness" (Isa. 26:9). God's love for His children means that He wants them to live and flourish in every way. His heart is inclined to bless, not curse them.

That is why God embedded a promise of deliverance in these first decrees of judgment. While throwing the serpent into the dust, the Lord said, "I will put enmity between you and the woman, and between your seed and her seed; He shall bruise you on the head, and you shall bruise Him on the heel" (Gen. 3:15). Theologians have called this statement the "protoevangelium," or "the first preaching of the Gospel." God declared *right in the midst of judgment* that one day the seed of the woman would crush the head of the enemy, implying that humans would be liberated from the serpent's grip.

What wonderful mercy! The same God who would never allow "the guilty to go unpunished," is the same God who reveals Himself as, "compassionate and gracious, slow to anger, and abounding in love and faithfulness, maintaining love to thousands, and forgiving wickedness, rebellion and sin" (Ex. 34:6-7, NIV). This is the glory of God's nature. As a perfect Father, He will uphold His righteousness while pouring out His mercy in abundance.

The Judgment on the Antediluvian World (GEN. 7:17–24)

MANY CENTURIES HAD PASSED SINCE THE JUDGMENT on Adam and Eve. And many centuries remained before the great judgment at the cross. But sin in the earth had reached a dangerous boiling point. "The Lord saw how great the wickedness of the human race had become and that every inclination of the thoughts of the human heart was only evil all the time. The Lord regretted that he had made human beings on the earth, and his heart was deeply troubled. So the Lord said, 'I will wipe from the face of the earth the human race I have created'" (Gen. 6:5-6, NIV).

The original creation had become too corrupt; it could not continue in its present state. God had to intervene. "Behold, I, even I am bringing the flood of water upon the earth, to destroy all flesh in which is the breath of life, from under heaven; everything that is on the earth shall perish" (Gen. 6:17). It seemed like absolute devastation. But in fact, this flood would act both as a comprehensive judgment *and* an act of extreme mercy! God could have just started over—creating a new world with new creatures. But instead, God found a man through whom He could redeem the human race and all of creation. "Noah found favor in the eyes of the Lord... Noah was a righteous man, blameless among the people of his time, and he walked faithfully with God" (Gen. 6:8-9, NIV). So his family, along with pairs of every kind of animal saved on the Ark, would represent a new beginning.

Out of the floodwaters of justice would arise a completely renewed creation. In fact, the floodwaters, in the end, *saved* creation from its own corruption. What a brilliant act of creative love working in tandem with perfect justice.

The Judgment of Man's Sin at the Cross (Isa. 53:4-8)

THERE IS NO GREATER MIXTURE OF JUDGMENT AND mercy than the crucifixion of Jesus Christ. It stands in continuity with former judgments, but still stands alone in its glory and significance. No judgment has ever accomplished God's justice, nor dispensed His wrath, like the cross. And neither has any judgment ever accomplished God's mercy, nor dispensed His salvation, like the cross. Let's take a closer look.

On Calvary, Jesus "was pierced through for our transgressions, He was crushed for our iniquities; the chastening for our well-being fell upon Him, and by His scourging we are healed" (Isa. 53:5). God's justice demanded a penalty. So Jesus took that penalty on our behalf *representing all of sinful humankind before the Lord* (Isa. 52:13-53:12). That is how "the iniquity of us all [could] fall on Him" (Isa. 53:6). It is how God "made Him who knew no sin to be sin on our behalf" (2 Cor. 5:21). And it is why God then "judged" Him. When God "crushed Him, putting Him to grief" as a sin offering (Isa. 53:10), He was judging all sin and all of sinful mankind. Behold the cross as God's massive judgment against an entire race!

But behold, too, His mercy! This same Servant of the Lord, after suffering for His people's sins, would then "see His offspring [...], prolong His days, and the good pleasure of the Lord will prosper in His hand" (Isa. 53:10). In fact, "as a result of the anguish of His soul, He will see it and be satisfied [...] My Servant will justify the many" (Isa. 53:11). In other words, Jesus would rise from the dead and enjoy the fruits of His sacrificial death! As the ultimate Man, if the Servant's *death* absorbed the judgment against humanity, then His resurrected *life* would effectively *renew* all who would believe.

So when we accept Jesus' sacrifice for ourselves, God does more than forgive us. He *renews* us with a whole new kind of life—a new creation. The Spirit of God that hovered over the waters at the beginning, and then helped renew creation during the Flood, now floods our hearts with new life. He makes us a whole new kind of humanity.

My friend, here we see the unparalleled glory and wisdom of the cross. It combines God's perfect justice with His perfect mercy. On the cross, God satisfied His own righteous nature by judging the sins of humanity. At the same time, He satisfied His own mercy by liberating everyone who believes. There is no religion or philosophy that compares to the wisdom and power of the cross! No other ideology could so completely deal with the depths of sin, so perfectly fulfill the demands of justice, and so wonderfully show mercy to sinners by offering them a whole new creation—*all in the same act!* Hallelujah!

The Great White Throne Judgment (Rev. 20:11–15)

SCRIPTURE TEACHES THAT ONE DAY, ALL THE DEAD will be raised—both believers and unbelievers—and they will all be judged (Dan. 12:2; John 5:28-29; Acts 24:15). But those who never received God's gift of salvation in Christ will be raised specifically to a resurrection of damnation. They will appear before the Great White Throne, be judged for their wicked deeds, and cast into the lake of fire (Rev. 20:13-15). This judgment is the ultimate act of God's justice, conclusively judging those who refused to believe. But it is also an act of mercy toward creation, when God forever cleanses the earth of sin.

I remember as a boy, hearing the preacher say, "If your sins aren't under the blood of Jesus, one day they will follow you to the judgment." I thought to myself,

"That must be an exaggeration. There is no possible way that God could have such a massive memory bank." But that occurred in my young mind before the days of the Internet, when computers were little more than glorified calculators. Things have changed since then, haven't they? Now it's easier to imagine God's colossal, all-inclusive database.

These days, I can almost discover people's entire life story just by visiting their Facebook pages or Twitter feeds. I can find out what they had for breakfast this morning and what they watched on television last night. You can find out where they were born, what they do for a living, what interests they have, and much more.

I'm sure you've heard that some search engines keep records of all your Internet searches and keystrokes. Imagine someone a hundred years from now investigating your life and getting hold of every search you did on the Internet, every website you visited, and all your social media pages—Facebook, Pinterest, YouTube and Twitter. They might know more about you than your own family members do. Yet God has a memory cache far more immense and precise than all the data banks on the planet put together. He will not need to subpoena your records from Google. He already has it all. And one day everyone will give an account.

A salacious bit of recent news offers a forewarning of that day. It featured a website that assists people to have adulterous affairs—the Ashley Madison website. Someone hacked the site and exposed 30 million people on the Internet—their names, addresses, and credit card numbers. The motto of the website was "Life is Short,

Have an Affair." Perhaps they need a new motto: "Be Sure Your Sins Will Find You Out."

"Do not be deceived, God is not mocked; for whatever a man sows, that will he also reap" (Gal. 6:7). There is coming a day, my friend—whether you get hacked or not —that all the sins not covered by the blood of Jesus will be exposed. In fact, the Bible tells us that, in that day, men will crawl under the rocks and they will ask the mountains to fall on them to hide them from the face of the One who sits upon the throne and from the wrath of the Lamb (Rev. 6:16). That day is coming. And for many, that is bad news.

The good news is that you do not have to appear at The Great White Throne Judgment. If you surrender your life to Jesus, His blood washes away your sins. He forgives you; He wipes your slate clean. *"There is now no condemnation to those who are in Christ Jesus"* (Rom. 8:1, NKJV).

I hope that, if you are not a believer, you will surrender your life to Jesus today. He loves you, died for you, and does not want you to carry the weight of your sin any longer. Jesus already took the judgment for your sins so you don't have to be judged for them. He took the penalty on your behalf on the cross. But, if you reject His offer to pay your debt, then you will have to pay for it yourself. That's the purpose of the Great White Throne Judgment.

To this point, our list of God's judgments should make a sober impression on our souls. It establishes that His judgments are *real*, they are just, and they are merciful. Even though believers will be spared the final judgment, we still live our lives before the One who, by His very nature of love and justice, evaluates all things. For believers, He is the One with whom we have to do. That is why even David said, "My flesh trembles for fear of You, and I am afraid of your judgments." And that is why Paul referred to a coming judgment *for believers* that produced in him "the fear of the Lord" (2 Cor. 5:11).

The Judgment Seat of Christ

AND SO WE COME TO THE LAST JUDGMENT OF THIS discussion: the Judgment Seat of Christ. We will spend the most time here because this is the judgment that will test the works of Christians. Even though true believers are exempt from God's judgment of *condemnation*, we are not exempt from His judgment of *evaluation*. The Bible teaches that our expectation of this future judgment helps us to live for the Lord in the present age. Paul calls such motivation, "the fear of the Lord" (2 Cor. 5:11).

As with all of God's judgments, the Judgment Seat of Christ perfectly blends His justice and His mercy. It displays justice because it brings our lives on earth into the light of eternity. The same respect God showed Adam's free will in the Garden, He will also show us at the end of the age. Our actions are important. How we live matters. True, God will not judge us for our sins before the cross. But He will evaluate our lives in light of the cross.

So let's look more closely at the Judgment Seat of Christ. Let's get ready for that just and merciful day. Our key text is 2 Corinthians 5. The rest of our study will focus on verses 10-20 along with a few other relevant passages. This will give us a better grasp of Paul's meaning, a richer understanding of the nature of God's judgment of Christians, and greater preparation for our future.

> *"We must all appear before the judgment seat of Christ, that each one may receive the things done in the body, according to what he has done, whether good or bad."*
> *(2 Corinthians 5:10, NKJV)*

The Greek word for "judgment seat" is *bēma*. In the world of the New Testament, *bēma* referred to a raised platform from which a speaker would address a crowd (Acts 12:21), or a ruler would make judgments on important legal matters. So a *bēma* usually referred to a tribunal—a judge's bench in a court of justice. Jesus Christ stood before the "judgment seat" (*bēma*) of Pontius Pilate (Matt. 27:19; John 19:13). Paul stood before Caesar's *bēma* (Acts 25:10-11), and testified before the *bēma* of the governor, Festus (Acts 25:6).

The ancient city of Corinth had a well-known *bēma* for legal matters, the remains of which survive to this day. In fact, Paul himself stood before that *bēma*. When Jews in Corinth accused him of leading a religious rebellion, they brought him before the *bēma*, or "judgment seat," of Gallio, who was the Roman governor of that province (Acts 18:12). So the Corinthians would understand well Paul's reference to the "judgment seat of Christ" in this verse (2 Cor. 5:10). It was no small matter to stand before the *bēma* of a judge, governor, or Roman Emperor! Verdicts there were weighty, binding, and final. Those who might stand before such judgment seats should take great care with their actions and their words. How much more, Paul suggests, should we believers live circumspectly since, one day, we will all stand before the *bēma* of the greatest and final Judge, King Jesus the Messiah? No wonder Paul admitted in the next verse that he "knew the fear of the Lord" (2 Cor. 5:11)!

But as I said earlier, the same judgment that gives us respect for God's justice, also invites us into His mercy. Interestingly, there was also a *bēma* at the Greek Olympic Games. But this "judgment seat" was not for trying law cases. It was for rewarding athletic competitors. The Corinthians would also have been familiar with this *bēma*. Some Olympic-type games were played right near their city every other spring when athletes from all over the Empire would converge on Corinth to challenge one another in various athletic events. After each contest, the winners would stand before a judge's *bēma* to receive the awards for their performances.

This *bēma* might also be a fitting illustration of Paul's point for two reasons. First, notice that only winners stand before the *bēma*. Just as in the Olympics today, losers do not receive medals. Everyone who stands before the *bēma* is a winner. If you make it to the Judgment Seat of Christ, it means you have been saved. You have been redeemed and will spend eternity with Jesus. That makes you a winner.

Second, however, there will be different levels among

The same judgment that gives us respect for God's justice, also invites us into His mercy.

these winners. Not every winner receives equal reward. This is not something we talk about very often in the church—because it is not politically correct. We live in a culture where everybody is supposed to be exactly equal. Even in many sport competitions for children, everyone gets medals and trophies so nobody feels left out. But in the real world, there are winners and there are losers. Even among champions, some do better than others and everyone is rewarded according to his or her work.

Remember what Paul said about those coming to this Judgment Seat: "We *must all appear...*" Notice he was not addressing heathens. He was speaking to the Corinthian church—believers who were Paul's own disciples. And he did not say, "You must all appear..." he included himself.

"We must all appear..." So even the great apostle, who spread the Gospel across the Mediterranean world and wrote two thirds of the New Testament, will in fact stand before the Judgment Seat of Christ himself. If the Corinthian believers have to face Christ's judgment seat, so do you. If the apostle Paul must face it, so must you. "*We* must *all* appear before the Judgment Seat of Christ..."

> If you make it to the Judgment Seat of Christ, it means you have been saved. You have been redeemed and will spend eternity with Jesus. That makes you a winner.

Notice also that he said we *"must"* all appear. There are no exceptions for extenuating circumstances. It isn't like jury duty where it is compulsory unless you have an acceptable excuse. There are no such exemptions from the

Judgment Seat of Christ. It is an appointment that cannot be cancelled. There are many uncertainties in this life. But I can tell you two things that are for sure. The Bible says that (1) it is appointed for men once to die, and (2) after this comes the judgment (Heb. 9:27). We will all die. And we will all face judgment—whether at the Judgment Seat of Christ or the Great White Throne.

Scripture goes on to say that each of us will receive what is due for the things done in the body. Paul makes this point with precision. There is no space for ambiguity. He is not speaking poetically about an intangible fantasy. He is not speaking in figures of speech just for immediate effect. Rather, he is speaking of something very real, very practical, and very certain.

He says we will account for "things"—that's tangible.

He says we will account for what is "done"—that's action.

He says we will account for what is done "in the body"—that's physical.

In other words, we will give an account for tangible things and real actions done in our physical bodies on earth.

My friend, this is real. How you live matters. What you do during your life matters. And you will give an account for it.

We will *all* give an account for the things done in the body—"whether good or bad"—a point that confuses many people. "Does this mean that we're going to answer for our sins again? Is God going to dredge up those sins from the bottom of the sea where He buried them, and thrust them back in our faces at the Judgment Seat of Christ?" Emphatically, unequivocally, and categorically: No. That would insult the Spirit of grace and the glory of the cross. It would contradict Scripture. Sins that God forgives—sins under the blood of Jesus Christ—are gone forever. You will never be judged for them again. God has cast them into the sea (Mic. 7:19). Isaiah says, "*You have cast all my sins behind your back*" (Isa. 38:17). Essentially, God is saying, "I have put those sins in a place where I will never see them again. They are gone and we are marching forward into a totally renewed view of your future!"

So then, what does Scripture refer to when it says that we will give an account for the things that we've done, *good or bad* (2 Cor. 5:10)? The Greek words translated "good" and "bad" in this passage are *agathos* and *phaulos.* In this context, these words do not refer only to morally good or bad deeds. Rather, they imply an evaluation of "beneficial" versus "worthless." This is a very important point. My friend, you can be saved, you can be forgiven, you can be on your way to heaven, *and still live for worthless things*—and many Christians do! It's

> You can be saved, you can be forgiven, you can be on your way to heaven, and still live for worthless things—and many Christians do!

so easy to get caught up with the cares of life, the day-to-day activities, the pointless amusements, and worthless distractions that consume the days, weeks, months, and years of our lives *yet have no eternal worth!*

Yes, we will all give an account one day. But this reckoning will not deal with individual sins already forgiven by God. Those sins are gone. No, we will give an account for the way we lived our lives as redeemed children of God—for the things we did with the time, opportunities and resources God put into our hands.

Remember the parable of the servants who were given talents by their master? When the master returned from his journey, he wanted an account of his investment in their lives. Then each received a reward according to what he had done (Matt. 25:14-30). It will be the same for us. Christ's Judgment Seat will not be like a kindergarten award ceremony where everyone receives the same reward so no one feels left out. No, some will receive more reward than others. And some will even be ashamed.

> Some will receive more reward than others. And some will even be ashamed.

In Revelation 22:12 (NKJV), Jesus said, *"Behold I am coming quickly and My reward is with Me, to give to everyone according to his work."* We must make this crucial distinction. When it comes to salvation, it's *not* about works at all. But when it comes to eternal rewards, it *is* all about works. It does matter what you do and it does matter how you live. In eternity, some are going to have greater status than others. That may sound unfair.

But do you think that someone like Mother Teresa who spent her whole life giving to the poor and sacrificing herself for others is going to receive the same reward as some guy who spent most of his life sitting on the couch playing Xbox? That would be unrighteous and our God is a righteous judge. Hebrews 6:10 says that God is not unjust; that *He will not forget your work* and the love that you have shown Him as you have helped His people and continue to help them. That means it would be unrighteous for God to forget your work.

The Scriptures are clear. God will reward each of us according to our work. And that day is close at hand. He is coming quickly and His reward is with Him. But what does that look like? What kind of rewards are these? How does this reward system operate?

At the ancient world's *bēma* for athletic games, competitors were rewarded in accordance with their performances. Even today, in the Olympics, winners stand on platforms of differing heights—the first place platform is higher than the second place, and second place is higher than the third. This is the picture that we get from Paul's language. One day, at the *bēma* of Christ, some will be rewarded in greater measure than others, based on the eternal value of their works.

We don't talk very much about these things, do we? We don't think often about

> When it comes to salvation, it's not about works at all. But when it comes to eternal rewards, it is all about works. It does matter what you do and it does matter how you live.

eternity. Our retirement plans, our investments and our physical fitness get a great deal of our time and attention. Yet these things are so fleeting.

Think about this: if you retire at 65 but live to be 80, that would mean you have 15 years to enjoy what you spent your life to gain. Then it's over. All that work, all that saving and investing and wise living—for what? You will expend all of that effort for a measly 15 years of reward. But in eternity—a thousand years from now, ten thousand years from now, a million years from now—you will still reap the rewards of the seeds you planted in this mortal life. How much thought have you given to your eternal "retirement plan?"

> How much thought have you given to your eternal "retirement plan?"

Remember Jesus' parable of the minas. The servant who increased his master's investment ten times, received authority over ten cities. The servant who increased his master's investment five times, received authority over five cities. And the servant who earned no interest at all, lost even the little investment he had to start. Reward in the age to come is not automatic, and we will not all be rewarded the same. So now is the time to invest!

Esau offers us another picture. Though he despised his birthright and relinquished the privilege to carry on his father's heritage, *he was still a son*. Esau did not forfeit his sonship, but he did forfeit his

> Esau did not forfeit his sonship, but he did forfeit his inheritance.

inheritance. There will be people in the age to come who will always be God's sons and daughters, but will have forfeited certain eternal rewards for temporal gain. The Scripture says of Esau that he could not get his inheritance back, though he sought it with many tears. For Christians too: on that Day, it will be too late to regain an inheritance we lost by wasting our time and energy in this age.

In the story of Esther, of all the virgins brought to the king's palace, only one was chosen. Only one ascended the throne. Scripture tells us that the other women remained a part of the king's house, *but only one became a queen.* What was different about Esther? Rather than focusing on herself in her preparations, she asked her caretaker how to please the king. She took his advice, and was chosen from among the others to be the king's bride. Likewise, the bride of Christ will be prepared by the will of God through the work of the Holy Spirit and will include those who have yielded their lives and submitted to Him and laid themselves down on the altar. God will form them and fashion them and purify them into a bride for Christ.

A Glimpse of Eternity

SO NOT EVERYONE WILL RECEIVE THE SAME REWARD in the age to come. Some believers will actually be closer in proximity to the throne of God than others. Some will receive special honor from Him in front of all creation. Listen closely to Jesus' own words. "Everyone who exalts himself will be humbled, *and he who humbles himself will be exalted...* When you give a luncheon or a dinner, do not invite your friends or your brothers or your relatives or rich neighbors, otherwise they may also invite you in return and that will be your repayment. But when you give a reception, invite the poor, the crippled, the lame, the blind, and you will be blessed, since they do not have the means to repay you; *for you will be repaid at the resurrection of the righteous"* (Luke 14:11-14, emphasis added).

In this world, self-promoting, proud people love to decorate themselves with status symbols—like cars and clothes—that distinguish them from others and demonstrate their wealth or power. But one day, God will decorate men and women with honor, wealth and power beyond anything this world has ever known. And I have a hunch that those most honored will be the unlikeliest of people. Something tells me that those whom God will honor are not the same people we would honor (Luke 16:15; 1 Cor. 1:26-28).

> I have a hunch that those most honored will be the unlikeliest of people. Something tells me that those whom God will honor are not the same people we would honor.

I daresay that the most decorated men and women in eternity will be people whose names we have never heard. Many will be the unseen servants who were faithful in the most humble of circumstances. There will be a little girl who laid her life down for the Gospel, refusing to deny the name of Jesus and remaining faithful until death. There will be grandmothers who spent decades on their knees interceding for lost loved ones. No one saw their sacrifices—the burdened prayers, the sleepless nights, the tears, the groaning—except God. But on that day, they will receive the reward for their labor, and will be honored before angels and saints. There will be Sunday school teachers, church nursery workers, and janitors. There will be people who fed the homeless, people who left home to serve in foreign lands, and people who gave finances to send others. There will be saints from every walk of life with various callings and gifts, who were simply faithful to the assignment God gave them. They were faithful with their resources, faithful with their time, and faithful with their abilities. They were obedient to God's call, and one day, they will receive their reward. If this isn't good news to you, perhaps you aren't living in light of eternity. But those that do live for the coming age are looking forward to His appearing because they know He has something for them. "Behold I am coming quickly *and My reward is with me.*"

The book of Revelation paints a striking picture of saints who sit on thrones, and receive power from God to judge (Rev. 20:4). This is not symbolic. They sit on actual thrones. They receive real authority to judge. They *rule all of creation* with King Jesus.

Please, give careful consideration to this message. Satan fell because he put his eyes on the throne of God and desired it. That was his ambition. Yes, he tempts people with much lesser things, like material success, cars, clothes, popularity, and political power. But Satan himself had his eyes set on something much greater— something carnal humanity knows nothing about. It is a prize much greater than anything ever imagined—the very throne of God. *That* is what the devil wanted. But he was banished from Heaven for coveting it. The very thing he desired and rebelled to acquire, is the very thing he will never attain. And yet, Jesus said, *you* can sit on My throne with Me! You can have something that will turn the devil himself green with envy!

> You can have something that will turn the devil himself green with envy!

How is this possible? Exactly because of what Jesus taught us: only the *meek* inherit the earth (Matt. 5:5). In other words, those faithful saints whose only ambition was to serve, not their own interests, but the interests of their great King, will inherit the very thing the devil raged to obtain. Likewise, the tycoons and moguls of this world, who spent their whole lives chasing earthly riches, will look up at the ones sitting with Christ. They will weep and say, "I've wasted my whole life searching for things that were dust in the wind, and I didn't even know it!"

Notice what Jesus promises to "those who overcome." They will:

- Eat of the tree of life (Rev. 2:7).
- Receive a crown of life (Rev. 2:10).
- Eat the hidden manna (Rev. 2:17).
- Receive a white stone bearing their new name that only they would know (Rev. 2:17).
- Receive authority over the nations (Rev. 2:26).
- Receive the morning star (Rev. 2:28).
- Wear white garments (Rev. 3:5).

- Become pillars in God's temple and never go out of it again (Rev. 3:12).
- Have written on their very persons God's name, the name of Jerusalem, and the new name of Jesus Christ (Rev. 3:12).
- Sit with Christ on His throne (Rev. 3:21).

This extraordinary life of the age to come is difficult to picture. Scripture describes it in powerful images, and its practical details are beyond me. But two things I do know: it is unspeakably more glorious than all the wealth of this world, and *you can choose to live for that age*. While most people are chasing new cars, bigger houses, a few pieces of "green paper," or a better looking body, others have decided they will chase eternal rewards and store up treasures in heaven. The moment you drive a new car off the lot, it depreciates. The first year, it could go down in value by twenty percent. But something tells me those white garments will never lose their value. I'm not sure what the morning star is, but I have a feeling it will never depreciate. Even after a million years, I don't think that ruling nations will ever get boring!

I don't know about you, but I want Jesus to tattoo His new name on me. I want to sit on a throne with Him. I want to eat from the tree of life. I want to wear a crown on my head. I don't want to be somewhere on the fringe of the holy city like Moses looking into the Promised Land, seeing it only from a distance. I want to be one of those "pillars" in the house of God that never has to go out. I want to live close to Him for all of eternity, able to gaze upon the One who sits upon the throne and on the Lamb forever.

Deeds, Works, and Treasures in Heaven

what are you living for? Whatever your answer is, *that* will be judged at the bēma of Christ.

MY FRIEND, WHAT ARE YOU living for? Whatever your answer is, *that* will be judged at the *bēma* of Christ. It is exactly what our main text in 2 Corinthians 5 is talking about. In fact, Paul elaborates on this same judgment in his other letter to the Corinthians with unique striking imagery. In 1 Corinthians 3:10-15 (NKJV) he says,

> "According to the grace of God which was given to me, as a wise master builder I have laid the foundation, and another builds on it. But let each one take heed how he builds on it. For no other foundation can anyone lay than that which is laid, which is Jesus Christ. Now if anyone builds on this foundation with gold, silver, precious stones, wood, hay, straw, each one's work will become clear; for the Day will declare it, because it will be revealed by fire; and the fire will test each one's work, of what sort it is. If anyone's work which he has built on it endures, he will receive a reward. **If anyone's work is burned, he will suffer loss; but he himself will be saved, yet so as through fire.**"

When our main text (2 Cor. 5) says in verse 10 that we will be judged for the "things done in the body," it's literally referring to our works—the things we did and the way we lived. Those are the actions that, according to 1 Corinthians 3, will be tested by fire. *What you do and how you live matters.*

We often emphasize that believers are saved by grace; we can do nothing to earn our salvation. And of course that is quite true. I'm an evangelist. My whole ministry is predicated on this glorious *good news.* I underscore, highlight, and affirm it with all my heart. According to Ephesians 2:8-9 (NKJV), *"By grace you have been saved through faith, and that not of yourselves; it is the gift of God, not of works, lest anyone should boast."*

The Scripture is clear. There is nothing you can do to add to the finished work of Jesus Christ on the cross of Calvary. He bought it. He paid for it. He delivered it. It's yours. You and I were fully immersed in depravity and rebellion, completely lost, totally undeserving of salvation, and absolutely incapable of performing any kind of religious work to earn it. But right at this point of complete hopelessness, God came to the rescue. He Himself provided for our salvation, at His expense, as a free gift. We cannot supplement it. We can only receive it by faith. That is why 1 Corinthians 3:15 (NIV) also says that, if a believer's

> The Scripture is clear. There is nothing you can do to add to the finished work of Jesus Christ on the cross of Calvary.

works are burned up, "He will suffer loss, *yet he himself will still be saved*—even though only as one escaping through the flames."

While works do not save us, our good works will reward us. Remember that Paul wrote these words at a time when people did not have insurance policies, credit cards, or money protected in bank accounts. All of their worldly wealth and assets were contained in their homes. If a rich man woke up in the middle of the night with the smell of smoke in this nostrils, ran from his house with only the shirt on his back, and watched his house burn to the ground, he would be watching everything of value in his life disappear right before his eyes. He would stand before that blazing inferno as poor as the beggar in the gutter, with all of his worldly wealth consumed by the flames. Paul says that it will be like this for many of God's people on the day they stand before the Judgment Seat of Christ. They themselves will be saved, but everything else will burn. Everything they spent their lives building and acquiring in this world will go up in smoke. They will enter eternity without the rewards Jesus promised to the faithful. Yes, they will still be saved, but "only as one escaping through the flames."

That's why Jesus taught His disciples to lay up treasures in Heaven. He didn't say, "I will lay up treasures for you." He told *us* to lay them up for ourselves. Salvation comes only by grace. But *rewards* are another matter. Let's revisit Ephesians 2:8-9, but this time let's keep it in context and read the next verse also:

For by grace you have been saved through faith, and that not of yourselves; it is the gift of God, not *of works, lest anyone should boast. **For we are His workmanship, created in Christ Jesus for good works, which God prepared beforehand that we should walk in them** (Ephesians 2:8-10, NKJV).*

So we were not saved by good works, but we were saved for good works! Works are not the means of our salvation, but they are the expected outcome of our salvation. "So then, my beloved, just as you have always obeyed, not as in my presence only, but now much more in my absence, work out your salvation with fear and trembling (Phil. 2:12). As Oswald Chambers emphasized, it is our responsibility to "work out what God works in." Freely, God worked salvation *into* us, and we will be judged by how we work it *out*.

The Whole Point

GOD SAVED YOU FOR A REASON. YOU WERE NOT SAVED to be a decorative knickknack on God's shelf, merely filling space in Heaven for eternity. God saved you for the eternal purpose in His heart before the foundation of the world. He has a plan for all of creation (Eph. 3:11), a plan for all of His people (Rom. 8:28-29), and a plan specifically for you (Eph. 2:10). If you and I don't fulfill that purpose, we cheat God and ourselves—and for that we will give an account before the *bēma* of Christ.

Functional Atheism

NOW LET'S RETURN TO OUR MAIN TEXT AND CONSIDER the following verses:

"Knowing, therefore, the terror of the Lord, we persuade men; but we are well known to God, and I also trust are well known in your consciences. For we do not commend ourselves again to you, but give you opportunity to boast on our behalf, that you may have an answer for those who boast in appearance and not in heart."
(2 Corinthians 5:11-12, NKJV)

Listen to that terminology: "The terror of the Lord." If those words do not make you very sober about the subject of eternity, I would suggest you are thinking like a fool. If you think my language is too strong, remember what the Bible itself says. *"The fool has said in his heart, 'There is no God'"* (Ps. 14:1).

You might respond: "Wait a minute: that verse refers to atheists, doesn't it? The atheist is a fool because he said in his heart there is no God. Right?" Not so fast. The atheist says with his *lips* there is no God. But the one who says in his *heart* "there is no God" may still profess with his lips that he believes in God. Yet the way he lives demonstrates that, deep down in his heart, he does not actually believe in eternity. The Judgment Seat of Christ and the reality of eternal reward have no practical bearing on his present life. If they did, he would live differently! This is what I call "functional atheism"—to say one thing with your mouth but to affirm something else with your life.

If this seems a little heavy, stay with me. The tone of the passage will change in a moment. But first Paul needs to show us how serious this is, and what is at stake. He would not do us a service if he minced words. Not only are there a Heaven to gain and a hell to shun, there are also rewards available to faithful Christians beyond our wildest dreams. So if we don't live in such a way that we store up treasures in Heaven, we are functional atheists thinking like fools and lacking what Paul calls the "terror of the Lord."

Listen to a story Leonard Ravenhill told about a man condemned to death.

Charlie Peace was a criminal. Laws of God or man curbed him not. Finally the law caught up with him, and he was condemned to death. On the fatal morning in Armley Jail, Leeds, England, he was taken on the death-walk. Before him went the prison chaplain, routinely and sleepily reading some Bible verses. The criminal touched the preacher and asked what he was reading. "The Consolations of Religion," was the reply.

Charlie Peace was shocked at the way he professionally read about hell. Could a man be so unmoved under the very shadow of the scaffold as to lead a fellow-human there and yet, dry-eyed, read of a pit that has no bottom into which this fellow must fall? Could this preacher believe the words that there is an eternal fire that never consumes its victims, and yet slide over the phrase without a tremor? Is a man human at all who can say with no tears, "You will be eternally dying and yet never know the relief that death brings?" All this was too much for Charlie Peace. So *he* preached. Listen to his on-the-eve-of-hell sermon.

"Sir," addressing the preacher, "if I believed what you and the church of God *say* that you believe, even if England were covered with broken glass from coast to coast, I would walk over it, if need be, on hands and knees and think it worthwhile living, just to save one soul from an eternal hell like that!"

So often, there is a profound disconnect between what we say we believe and how we live in response to those beliefs. I pray that even through this booklet, your whole life would be refocused to live for the *bēma* of Christ! Faith does not merely accept that God *is*, but also that *He is a rewarder* of those who diligently seek Him (Heb. 11:6).

> *"For the love of Christ compels us, because we judge thus: that if One died for all, then all died" (v. 14, NKJV)*

Faith does not merely accept that God is, but also that He is a rewarder of those who diligently seek Him.

Imagine a death row inmate who is just about to be executed. He has just eaten his last meal. The electric chair is warmed up and ready. Suddenly someone knocks on the door. It's a pardon from the governor. This man—as good as dead a few moments ago—has now been released. He's been given his life back. This sort of story has often been used to illustrate our salvation. But when it comes to what Jesus did for us on the cross, it goes so much deeper. When we were rescued from eternal death, the Governor did not merely send a pardon. He entered the execution chamber, sat in the electric chair Himself, and took the execution we deserved as prisoners on eternal death row. Paul's point is that Jesus exchanged His life for ours. Are you living your life for Him? Love begets love and His sacrifice should kindle a desire to sacrifice in us. Paul continues with the same thought in the next verse...

He died for all that, those who live should live no longer for themselves, but for Him who died for them and rose again. (v. 15, NKJV)

As Leonard Ravenhill asked: "Are the things you're living for worth Christ dying for?" Do you evaluate your life and your priorities in light of the price Jesus paid for you? The natural response might be, "Well, it's my life. I can live how I want to live." No, my friend, it's not your

> "Are the things you're living for worth Christ dying for?"

life. You have been bought with a price and your life is not your own, "therefore, glorify God in your body" (1 Cor. 6:20).

I love to tell this story when I preach the gospel in Africa. It's the true account of an old Baptist pastor from the 1800s, preparing his Sunday sermon on Saturday afternoon. After several hours of study, he got tired and went for a walk to stretch his legs. As he walked through town, he saw a boy carrying a birdcage in one hand and a stick in the other. Inside the cage were a dozen little field birds, and the boy was jabbing the birds through the bars with the stick. The birds were shrieking, feathers were flying, and the boy was laughing. The pastor approached the boy. "Son," he said, "why are you tormenting those birds?"

The boy said, "Sir, I love to hear them shriek. I love to see their feathers fly. It is so much fun."

"What will you do when you are finished having your fun?" the pastor asked.

The boy smiled broadly. "Oh sir, that's the best part. I will bring them home, take them out of the cage one by one, pluck their feathers, and feed them to my cat."

The pastor's heart was broken. "Son, let me have those birds," he said.

"No, these are my birds. I caught them myself. You can get your own birds. You can catch some in the field."

"But I want those birds."

"Why? They don't even sing. They aren't canaries, you know. They are just ordinary field birds."

"Please, son. I'll buy them from you. How much do you want?"

The pastor took out his wallet and opened it up. Suddenly the boy saw a business opportunity. "How much money do you have, sir?" The pastor counted two dollars, which was a lot of money in those days.

"What a coincidence," the boy said. "They cost exactly two dollars, cage included."

The pastor knew the boy was ripping him off, but he took all the money out of his wallet and handed it to the boy. The next day the pastor told this story as he stood before his congregation. He said, "I took that cage out into the field. I opened the door and I backed away. One by one the birds hopped to the open door. One by one they spread their wings, and one by one they began to fly. And as they flew to freedom they began to sing the same song. And this was their song: 'Redeemed, Redeemed, Redeemed.'"

This is what Jesus has done for us. When God looked down on a world full of helpless souls trapped in the prison of sin—tormented by fears and tears, by addictions and compulsions—His heart was moved with compassion. He knew that we could do nothing to save ourselves and He knew that without His deliverance, we would spend eternity in hell. This does not mean that God made a deal with the devil. I don't believe any such thing. But it does mean that God truly "redeemed" us from our bondage.

The word "redeemed" in the New Testament means to liberate by the payment of a ransom. But what was the price of our ransom? Peter tells us explicitly: "For you know that it was not with perishable things such as silver or gold that you were redeemed from the empty way of life handed down to you from your ancestors, but with the precious blood of Christ, a lamb without blemish or defect" (1 Pet. 1:18-19, NIV).

We have been redeemed. We have been purchased—not with dollars or Euros, not with silver or gold. In fact, the currency God used to purchase your redemption was the most precious substance in the universe—the very blood of Jesus Christ. When God purchased your salvation, Heaven went bankrupt. For even the streets of gold are worthless by comparison to the blood of God's eternal Son. God could create a whole new universe with a word. But only that precious blood of Jesus Christ could redeem our souls. So Paul says, "Those who live should no longer live for themselves, but for Him who died for them and rose again!" The next verse takes it even further.

Who He Is, Who I Am

Therefore, from now on, we regard no one according to the flesh. Even though we have known Christ according to the flesh, yet now we know Him thus no longer. (v. 16, NKJV)

THERE WAS A TIME WHEN EVEN JESUS' DISCIPLES didn't realize who He was. They saw Him as a good man, prophet, or teacher. But after His glorious resurrection, they discovered the enormous part of His identity they had missed. He was so much bigger and so much greater than what they had perceived with their natural senses. Jesus Christ was God Himself. So Paul says that we should not make that mistake again. In fact, from now on, we should not view anyone in Christ as a normal human. Jesus has made us more than ordinary people. He has created us as part of the divine family. The Bible speaks often about our true identity as God's people in Christ. We...

Have been resurrected from the dead with Christ (Col. 3:1).
Are the expression of Christ's divine life (Col. 1:4).
Are chosen, holy, and loved by God (Col. 3:12).

Are children of the light (1 Thess. 5:5).

Have a heavenly calling (Heb. 3:1).

Are sons and daughters of God (Gal. 3:26).

Are God's temple (1 Cor. 3:16).

Have been bought with a price (1 Cor. 6:20).

Have been raised with Christ and seated in
heavenly places (Eph. 2:6).

Have been set free from sin (Rom. 6:18).

Are the aroma of Christ (2 Cor. 2:15).

Are the light of the world (Matt. 5:14).

Have been sealed by the Holy Ghost (2 Cor. 1:22).

Are joint heirs of God with Christ (Rom. 8:17).

Are anointed (2 Cor. 1:21).

Have been born again of imperishable seed
(1 Pet. 1:23).

This is how you and I should be regarded, Paul said. If you have embraced Christ, you are liberated from your sinful state and plunged into an entirely new identity in Christ. So if I am teaching you or conversing with you, I'm going to talk to you as the son or daughter of God that you really are.

On the other hand, when I preach the gospel at an evangelistic campaign, I don't talk like this because I am talking to people who are unsaved and unregenerate. They are still in their sins. They need the message of salvation by grace through

Dead men can do nothing. A dead man can't be asked to do good works. But when God breathes His new life into you, He can then require something of you.

faith. But believers know that salvation is not the finish line. It's the starting line.

As a believer, you have been raised to a new, divine life with Christ. You have the ability now to live a holy life. You have the ability to do good works. You have the power to *live* in the truest, most biblical sense of that word. **Dead men can do nothing.** A dead man can't be asked to do good works. But when God breathes His new life into you, He can then require something of you. And it is in this context that in the next verse Paul expresses this well-known passage—this piece of biblical gold that every Christian knows by heart.

> *"Therefore, if anyone is in Christ, he is a new creation; old things have passed away; behold, all things have become new. (v. 17, NKJV)*

This is too wonderful for words! The old you has died and was buried with Christ. That person, so full of lust and pride, is dead. That person who was a guilty sinner is gone. That person who was defined by people's opinions or former abuses, who always felt inadequate, who always felt like a disappointment, who walked around with an orphan spirit, who was a slave to sin... That selfish, lazy, hateful, arrogant, undisciplined, unholy person has disappeared forever. He died. The old *is gone*—and the new has indeed come. You are now a new kind of human, made in God's image, and capable of doing extraordinary good works. He is for you, not against you. He loves you, and as a Father, He wants the best for your life. Now we can rise up, wake up, and fulfill His destiny for us. How wonderful! How glorious! But Paul doesn't stop there. He goes on to more wonderful things still...

A Powerful New Vocation

Now all things are of God, who has reconciled us to Himself through Jesus Christ, and has given us the ministry of reconciliation. (v. 18, NKJV)

NOT ONLY HAS GOD RECONCILED US TO HIMSELF through Christ, He has also given us the ministry of reconciliation—a service to bring people back to God! Have you ever had a bad quarrel with someone you loved? Maybe you didn't talk to each other for a few days afterward. Do you remember what that felt like? Your heart was painfully heavy. The whole world seemed overcast and gloomy as long as that schism remained.

But do you remember what it felt like when you reconciled? Life returned and your heart felt "born again." Relationships are very powerful. When they are broken, the sun goes down. But reconciliation brings a new day. This is what happened when God reconciled with the human race. Even though the schism was entirely the fault of humanity, God initiated reconciliation with us! We caused the split, putting God on the receiving end of our wickedness and rebellion. Yet it was He who gave Himself up, making Himself vulnerable to further rejection and abuse from us—all to become our Friend.

And while most of the world has refused Him, a few of us have seen His outstretched arms. Something inside of us broke. We came to Him, and were reconciled to Him. Then, in the most dramatic, divine, miraculous, and powerful way possible, the sun rose again and new life returned to our hearts. The reconciliation of *this* relationship made us born again! What a wonderful reality! We are no longer enemies of God! We are His friends—close, intimate friends. We have been brought near through the precious blood of Jesus Christ.

But once we are brought near to the living God, the life-giving power of that reconciliation comprises more than a new friendship. It empowers us to become *ministers* of reconciliation. Put another way, we are qualified to become ministers of reconciliation, not when a church ordains us, but when God reconciles us!

Usually when people hear the word "minister," they think of an ordained, full-time preacher. But when I travel internationally, and customs officials ask for my occupation, I tell them, "I am a minister." Their follow up question is, "A minister of what?" They assume if I am a minister, I work for a government. To them, the word "minister" means an agent, representative, or ambassador. In fact, that is the proper meaning of the word. So yes, I am a minister—not because I am ordained as a full-time preacher, but because I work for God's government in the department of reconciliation. And so do you! We got our jobs when we were reconciled to God. Now we are called to bring others into the same renewed friendship of reconciliation to God in Christ, and that leads us to the next verse.

God was in Christ reconciling the world to Himself, not imputing their trespasses to them, and has committed to us the word of reconciliation. (v. 19, NKJV)

Paul elaborates on this ministry of reconciliation. Not only did God *qualify* us to become His ministers, but He also *entrusted* us with the message of reconciliation. That means we have both the privilege *and* responsibility to share the "word" of reconciliation.

It is exciting to think about being ministers in God's department of reconciliation. But it is also sobering—because it is our duty. When a president or king sends a minister to another country, he does not send him on a vacation. The cost of the jet, fuel, pilots, attendants, food, lodging, and salary are all investments in the diplomacy between the two countries. What would happen if a king's minister used his role merely to travel and party in new places? Such an envoy may have qualified for his job in the past. But now he is not being faithful to his job. He's using it for his own benefit, rather than the benefit of his country and king.

Likewise, when we became ministers of reconciliation in v. 18, Paul explains that we were also *entrusted* with that ministry in v. 19. God blessed us with the honor of our new role when we became friends. But He also expects us to fulfill that role. In context, then, Paul is telling us that, if

> The ministry of reconciliation has indeed become the context for the good works to be judged on that final day.

we want to live in light of the *bēma* seat of Christ, we must take up our responsibility as His ambassadors with full reliability. The ministry of reconciliation has indeed become the context for the good works to be judged on that final day.

A Powerful New Message

Now then, we are ambassadors for Christ, as though God were pleading through us: we implore you on Christ's behalf, be reconciled to God. (v. 20, NKJV)

As Christ's ambassadors, our message is urgent. Notice Paul's pressing language. God is "pleading" through us. That means He is appealing, urging, and exhorting people with the intensity of someone who sees imminent danger that others may not see. And he says we "implore" people. That word means to request with earnestness, or even beg. There is no avoiding the vivid, almost desperate tone of this verse. Reconciliation with God is wonderful, but it is also imperative. The dangers of humanity's broken relationship with God are enormous. Reconciliation is essential! The Great White Throne Judgment is the final and everlasting judgment on unbelieving humankind. Therefore, God's reconciled friends have become His agents of reconciliation—His ambassadors of peace—to warn people earnestly and beg them to return to their God.

But here's the irony. In context, we ministers appeal earnestly to people, not only because *they* are heading to judgment, but also because *we* are heading to judgment. We will appear before a throne of rewards to determine the quality of our eternal existence. That should motivate us to work for reconciliation now! Just as a king's ambassador will have to return home and face his king and give an account, so we will all appear before the *bēma* of Christ, that is, before the judgment seat of the Messiah-King of Israel and Lord of all nations.

The Emphasis on Judgment in Paul's Writings

SO FAR WE HAVE SPENT MOST OF OUR TIME IN 1 AND 2 Corinthians, but the theme of Christ's Judgment Seat is not confined to these two letters. Once awakened to this theme, it is hard to read even one page of the New Testament without seeing it plainly, or feeling its influence. The apostle Paul, who wrote two thirds of the New Testament, repeatedly referred to judgment one way or another. He spoke often of "That Day." In fact, most of his references to the Lord's return occur in the context of a returning Judge to whom we will give an account, and include a call to live in light of that day. Paul writes his letters from the perspective of a sentinel keeping the last watch of the night. The dawn of the Lord's return and judgment is just about to break. Its light will soon turn night to day and saturate creation with its all-seeing radiance. Anticipation of that moment so pervades Paul's

> Anticipation of that moment so pervades Paul's worldview, that we simply cannot grasp his message without it.

worldview, that we simply cannot grasp his message
without it.

- In Romans, Paul mentions that day often. In
  chapter two, he speaks of the "day of wrath"—a
  coming day when God's righteous judgment
  will be revealed and He "will render to each one
  according to his deeds" (Rom. 2:5-6).
- Later, he addresses believers, contrasting "the
  sufferings of this present time" with the "glory
  that is to be be revealed to us" (Rom. 8:18).
- In chapter 13, Paul challenges the Romans to
  holy living by reminding them that, "the night is
  almost gone, and the day is near" (Rom. 13:12).
- Likewise, in the next chapter he warns them
  not to pass judgment against their brothers by
  reminding them that, "we will all stand before
  the judgment seat [*bēma*] of God" (Rom. 14:10).

As we have already seen, Paul's two letters to the
Corinthians are full of exhortations to live in light of
the coming day of judgment. For Paul, *everything* about
church life should relate specifically to the imminent
day of the Lord. Paul even sees charismatic gifts as one
way the church expresses its eager expectancy of "the
revelation of our Lord Jesus Christ" (1 Cor. 1:7)—the day
he believes the Corinthians will be judged as "blameless in
the day of our Lord Jesus Christ" (1 Cor. 1:8).

Throughout the rest of 1 Corinthians, Paul sets the
final Day of Judgment before the Corinthians to motivate
them to...

Build the church (1 Cor. 3:12-17)
Stop criticizing his leadership (1 Cor. 4:5)
Discipline a sinful church member (1 Cor. 5:5)
Settle legal disputes (1 Cor. 6:9-10)
Walk in sexual purity (1 Cor. 6:14)
Live free from worldly ambition (1 Cor. 7:29-31)
Exercise self-control for the gospel (1 Cor. 9:23-27)
Partake worthily of the Lord's Supper (1 Cor. 11:26)
Love one another (1 Cor. 13:10, 13),
And do the Lord's work (1 Cor. 15:58).

In fact, all of chapter 15 puts the inspiration for our present life in the context of the Lord's return (15:23), the resurrection (15:23), the end of time (15:24), and the renewal of all creation (15:28).

This same rhythm continues in 2 Corinthians. Paul finds deep wells of courage to preach the Gospel under duress, because one day he will be raised from the dead and be presented with his converts (2 Cor. 4:14). Then, on that day he will inherit an "eternal weight of glory far beyond all comparison" (2 Cor. 4:17). That is why Paul fixes his eyes only on "eternal" things (2 Cor. 4:18). In the next chapter, which we considered at such length in this book, Paul restates the reasons for his great gospel courage: one day he will stand before Christ's *bēma*, receive an immortal "tent," and be repaid for the deeds he did in his body (2 Cor. 5:1-11).

In Philippians 3:14, Paul talks about his efforts to press on for the prize of God's "upward call." Put another way, Paul wanted to "attain to the resurrection of the dead" (Phil. 3:11). This is in contrast to those phony gospel preachers "who set their minds on earthly things" (Phil. 3:19). In context, that means such ministers do not conduct their lives in view of the coming judgment day. But Paul and his comrades are different. They look forward to the day when Jesus "will transform the body of our humble state into conformity with the body of His glory, by the exertion of the power that He has even to subject all things to Himself" (Phil. 3:21). Paul calculated everything about his ministry, both motives and actions, backwards: from the Day of Judgment to his present life.

> Paul calculated everything about his ministry, both motives and actions, backwards: from the Day of Judgment to his present life.

In Ephesians and Colossians, Paul reminds servants, slaves and masters that they will give an account to their Master in heaven who judges with impartiality (Eph. 6:5-9; Col. 3:24-25).

In 1 Thessalonians, Paul expresses his joy for those believers because they will be his "proud reward and crown as we stand before our Lord Jesus Christ when He returns" (1 Thess. 2:19). Paul goes on to encourage them to live soberly and alertly so that "the day of the Lord... would [not] overtake you like a thief" (1 Thess. 5:2, 4, 6).

In 2 Thessalonians, Paul comforts Christians who suffer persecution. But the way he offers such comfort reveals a way of thinking that differs greatly from so much of this-worldly thinking among some Christians today. Paul does not tell his church that the world will eventually become a friendly place for Christians. Nor does he prophesy that their enemies will be judged anytime soon. Rather, he reminds them that God will judge their enemies in the future, "when the Lord Jesus will be revealed from heaven with His mighty angels in flaming fire, dealing out retribution to those...who do not obey the gospel of our Lord Jesus...when He comes to be glorified in His saints on that day" (1:7-10).

In 1 Timothy, Paul challenges those who are rich in this world not to trust in their riches, but to use them to store up treasures "for the age to come" (1 Tim. 6:19, HCSB). Then in the next epistle, Paul orders Timothy to proclaim the truth to the church in Ephesus with diligence and faithfulness. But notice the basis for his command. "I solemnly charge you in the presence of God and of Christ Jesus, who is to judge the living and the dead, and by His appearing and His kingdom: preach the word" (2 Tim. 4:1-2). Again, as far as Paul is concerned, Timothy should discharge his current ministry under the influence of future judgment.

Then, in that same vein, Paul speaks of his own death in that famous passage: "I have fought a good fight, I have finished my course, I have kept the

> I Have fought a good fight, I have finished my course, I have kept the faith: henceforth there is laid up for me a crown of righteousness, which the Lord, the righteous judge, shall give me at that day: and not to me only, but unto all them also that love his appearing (NASB).

faith: henceforth there is laid up for me a crown of righteousness, which the Lord, the righteous judge, shall give me at that day: and not to me only, but unto all them also that love his appearing" (2 Tim. 4:7-8).

In the book of Titus, Paul challenges us to deny ungodliness and worldly lusts—to live soberly, righteously, and godly in this present age. Why? Because we are "looking for that blessed hope and the glorious appearing of the great God and our Savior Jesus Christ" (Titus 2:11-14). looking for the blessed hope and the appearing of the glory of our great God and Savior, Christ Jesus (NASB)

> ...Looking for that blessed hope and the glorious appearing of the great God and our Savior Jesus Christ (NASB).

This is only a small sampling from Paul's writings to demonstrate the extent to which he saw life as a prelude to eternity. Yet this short list is still overwhelming, and its implications for us are profound. I can't help but wonder how many pastors and preachers today would deeply and practically agree with Paul. So often modern leaders shy away from even mentioning judgment. Yet Paul not only declares it clearly, but also stresses it often to give his churches hope, warning, and motivation. Actually, we cannot adequately preach

> We cannot adequately preach Paul's doctrine if we avoid teaching on the impending day of the Lord's judgment.

Paul's doctrine if we avoid teaching on the impending day of the Lord's judgment.

Judgment in the Other Epistles

BUT PAUL WAS BY NO MEANS ALONE. HE DID NOT invent the concept of the Judgment Seat of Christ. The other epistles are replete with references to the coming day of judgment—specifically judgment for believers.

The writer of Hebrews reminds his congregation that, "It is appointed unto men to die once, but after this the judgment" (9:27, NKJV). And in case there is any confusion, he strongly reinforces the idea one chapter later: "The Lord will judge his people" (10:30). Then the author praises the church because in persecution they had "accepted joyfully the seizure of your property, knowing that you have for yourselves a better possession and a lasting one" (10:34). He goes on to encourage them not to throw away their confidence because it will be greatly rewarded when Christ returns (10:35-38).

But the most profound vision of the coming judgment in Hebrews, and one of the clearest in the whole New Testament, we find it in the great "Hall of Faith" in chapter 11. So often this "Faith Chapter" is seen as an encouragement to have faith for things now. And that is certainly legitimate. But a closer reading fixes much of faith's reward in the future. To put our faith in God, according to Hebrews, is to believe in His present reality *as well as His future rewards*. In fact, if we do not believe that God will reward our faith in the future, we do not have faith that pleases Him (Heb. 11:6).

We learn here that "faith is the assurance of things hoped for" (Heb. 11:1). The Old Testament heroes who died in faith believed for an inheritance they never obtained while alive. They "desire[d] a better country, a heavenly one" (11:16). Their faith then becomes an example for Christians who, like Abraham, are "looking for the city which has foundations, whose architect and builder is God" (11:10). Yes, we approach God's mountain now by faith (12:22-24). But we also wait for a future day when all of creation will be shaken, and only God's unshakable Kingdom will remain (12:25-29). That is why the author exhorts his weary church to endure some pain now in light of the coming joy (12:1-3).

The book of James speaks clearly about God's judgment of His people. It opens with a blessing for those who endure temptation because, when they have been approved, they "will receive the crown of life" (James 1:12). James also warns people not to take the role of a teacher too hastily—for teachers will receive a stricter judgment (James 3:1). Then he warns Christians to stop grumbling against one another "so that you yourselves may not be judged; behold, the Judge is standing right at the door" (James 5:9).

The same theme continues to flow like a stream through Peter's and John's epistles. First Peter speaks of the day when God will judge the living and the dead (1 Peter 4:5). Second Peter describes the "Day of the Lord" in great detail (2 Pet. 3:10-13). First John talks about the boldness we can have in the Day of Judgment if we are "made perfect in love" (1 John 4:17). And Second John urges us to, "Watch yourselves, that you do not lose what we have accomplished, but that you may receive a full reward" (2 John 8).

Even the little book of Jude, only one chapter long, speaks of the coming of the Lord "with […] thousands of His saints, to execute judgment on all…" (Jude 1:14-15).

And of course, as we have already seen, the book of Revelation contains some of the most striking and vivid imagery of the coming judgment in all of Scripture. It declares that Jesus is coming quickly, He will judge the whole world, saint and sinner alike, and will establish His glorious Kingdom on earth.

Judgment in the Teachings of Jesus

BUT PERHAPS THE MOST WELL KNOWN REFERENCES TO judgment come from Jesus Himself. He taught about the "mystery" of God's Kingdom (Mark 4:11). The "mystery" means that the Kingdom had indeed come to earth through Him, but that it had not yet fully come. Those who repented and believed could enter it and experience its rich, spiritual life now. But there is

> Perhaps the most well known references to judgment come from Jesus Himself.

an even greater day coming when people least expect it. So Jesus teaches His disciples to get ready. He urges them how to live in anticipation of the Kingdom's future manifestation: when the King returns, the dead are raised, the wicked are judged, and the righteous are rewarded.

Even before Jesus appeared to Israel, John the Baptist prepared His way by warning people of "the wrath to come" and the fires of God's judgment (Matt. 3:7-12). Then once Jesus began to preach publicly, His messages were saturated with references to coming judgment.

In His "Sermon on the Mount," Jesus emphasizes future rewards as motivation for righteous living in the present age (Matt. 6:4, 6, 18). He teaches His disciples not to store up temporary "treasures on earth," but to store up eternal "treasures in heaven" (6:19-20). Then when Jesus warns against false prophets, He also warns of eternal judgment—away from His presence—for those who know His name and claim to work miracles, but who still fail to do "the Father's will" (7:19-23). Indeed, Jesus frames this entire Sermon within the brackets of future rewards (5:3-11) and future judgments (7:21-27).

When Jesus sends His disciples to preach in the cities and villages of Israel, He uses the coming judgment to bring the gravity of their mission into focus. If any city rejects their message, "it will be more tolerable for the land of Sodom and Gomorrah in the day of judgment than for that city" (Matt. 10:15; 11:24). He tells them they will be persecuted, but again points them to the last judgment to deter their fear. "Do not fear those who kill the body but are unable to kill the soul; but rather fear Him who is able to destroy both soul and body in hell" (Matt. 10:28). The world will not be friendly to them. Jesus' message will bring a sword, not peace (Matt. 10:34-36). But they are able to endure the world's rejection if they keep their minds on the future rewards of the coming age (Matt. 10:37-42).

Jesus' parables especially make this point clear: there is a judgment day coming at "the end of the age" (Matt. 13:40). Both disciples and sinners should be warned. In the parable of the wheat and tares, for example, the evil ones will be "gathered up and burned with fire… In that place there will be weeping and gnashing of teeth. Then the righteous will shine forth as the sun in the kingdom of their Father" (Matt. 13:40-43). Likewise, the parable of the dragnet uses good and bad fish to illustrate that "at the end of the age the angels will come forth and take out the wicked from among the righteous, and will throw them into the furnace of fire; in that place there will be weeping and gnashing of teeth" (13:49-50).

> Jesus' parables especially make this point clear: there is a judgment day coming at "the end of the age".

> Both disciples and sinners should be warned.

Near the end of His ministry—with apocalyptic language, sober tone, and yet more parables—Jesus forewarns His disciples about His awesome return and inescapable judgment. "The powers of the heavens will be shaken. And … they will see the Son of Man coming on the clouds of the sky with power and great glory" (Matt. 24:29-30). Summer's fig trees, Noah's flood, and a thief in the night warn disciples to recognize the season of the Lord's return, its sudden and shocking nature, and the impartiality of His judgment (Matt. 24:32-35; 24:36-41). The five foolish virgins learn (and teach) the same lesson

(Matt. 25:1-13). The bridegroom's delay puts the present age under the spotlight of coming judgment. The Lord's point? Be ready. Judgment is real, and it's coming.

Jesus' parables about the servants point His disciples to the Day of Judgment (Matt. 24:45-51; 25:14-30). The story's masters give their servants resources to use, and duties to perform, while they go away. During the delay, some servants serve faithfully and some act lazily. The faithful receive rewards; the wicked are cast into "the outer darkness; in that place there will be weeping and gnashing of teeth." Again, it is impossible to avoid Jesus' clear message—judgment is coming; live accordingly.

Finally, the parable of the sheep and the goats casts the bright light of future judgment on present life. Jesus cannot be more explicit. The Son of Man will come in glory with His angels. Then He will sit as King and Judge "on His glorious throne" (Matt. 25:31). The nations will gather before Him, and He will judge them based on their deeds—specifically, the way they treated Him through "these brothers of Mine, even these least of them" (Matt. 25:40, 45). Those who faithfully serve the King by serving His needy ones, will be judged like this: "Come, you who are blessed of My Father, inherit the kingdom prepared for you from the foundation of the world" (Matt. 25:34). Those who ignore the needy ones will be judged this way: "Depart from Me, accursed ones, into the eternal fire which has been prepared for the devil and his angels" (Matt. 25:41).

Jesus' teaching on judgment is as inescapable as the coming judgment itself. With frequency, consistency, and urgency, Jesus proclaims the future judgment, and urges

His listeners to live for that day. Disciples will be judged. Wicked people will be judged. Nations will be judged. Even angels will be judged. This is not theory, and it is not fiction. That is why Jesus Himself taught it so often and from so many angles.

If future judgment is such an important issue to the Master, should not His disciples take it seriously in their daily lives, and His shepherds preach it urgently? It is amazing to me that this theme of the Judgment, so central to Paul's teaching, so fundamental to the other New Testament authors and so emphasized by our Lord Jesus Himself is virtually non-existent in modern preaching. Although I am not a fan of angry "Hellfire and brimstone" type messages, I believe we have a duty to preach what is true without compromise. As teachers, we will receive a stricter judgment according to James 3:1. If we fail to prepare the saints for the Judgment Seat of Christ, we will answer for our neglect when we stand before it.

> If future judgment is such an important issue to the Master, should not His disciples take it seriously in their daily lives, and His shepherds preach it urgently?

At Last

So Paul returns to the theme of the *bēma* at the end of his life. Just before his death —just before he lays down his life, beheaded for the gospel—he writes:

"I have fought the good fight, I have finished the race, I have kept the faith. Finally, there is laid up for me the crown of righteousness, which the Lord, the righteous Judge, will give to me on that Day, and not to me only but also to all who have loved His appearing" (2 Tim. 4:7-8, NKJV).

As Paul faced the sword about to remove his head, he knew that his next stop would be the *bēma* of Christ. And there the Lord would give him a crown, awarding him for the work that he had done. What a shining example of a faithful life. Paul had no fear of death, because he had no fear of judgment. In fact, he *anticipated* judgment because he knew he did his best. He lived for eternity, and so he expected what the Lord had promised: glorious reward. How wonderful it would be if, at the end of your life, you don't have to be in fear or in dread of the judgment that is to come. You can say with Paul: "I have fought the good fight, I have run the race, I have kept the faith. Now there is a crown laid out for me. I am triumphant in Christ!"

Therefore we also, since we are surrounded by so great a cloud of witnesses, let us lay aside every weight, and the sin which so easily ensnares us, and let us run with endurance the race that is set before us, looking unto Jesus, the author and finisher of our faith, who for the joy that was set before Him endured the cross, despising the shame, and has sat down at the right hand of the throne of God (Heb. 12:1-2, NKJV).

What holds you back and keeps you from running the race? What weights keep you from living for eternity? What sins threaten your rewards? None of them is necessary. From within you, be empowered by your new identity in Christ. All around you, be encouraged by the great cloud of witnesses who lived in light of eternity. And before you, be inspired by the rewards of faithful service to the King. But also be sobered: on that Day we will all give an account for our deeds done in the body.

So do not let even good things become hindrances to eternal things. Eternity is too important to risk for the sake of some silly temporal thing that ultimately won't matter. Stop messing around. How you live matters. How you spend your time matters. How you serve the Lord matters. He is watching. He is noticing. He is keeping records and, one day, you will give an account. We will all give an account.

May you live your life from this day forward in the light of eternity. May you hear those words from the Master on that Day: "Well done my good and faithful servant..."

* * * *

I'd like to encourage you to take a moment and ask the Lord what is hindering you and limiting your investment in eternity. Pray along these lines:

"Father, I thank You that Your plans for me are perfect. Lord Jesus, I can never thank You enough for rescuing me from eternal death. Holy Spirit, I thank You for Your abiding, guiding presence. Search me

and try me. See if there is any wicked way in me. Show me where I have neglected eternal things and lived for temporary things. Show me the weights and sins that so easily beset me and keep me from running the race you've called me to run. Help me to live the kind of life that anticipates the Judgment Seat of Christ. I want all You have for me in this age, and in the age to come. Help me to fulfill Your intended purpose for my life. I surrender all to You, in Jesus' name.

Live Before You Die
The Experience

New video series by Daniel Kolenda.
3 DVD set with 7 dynamic
episodes and book.

ISBN: 9781933446301   SKU: KTEN044
$50.00

Raised from the Dead – Book and DVD Pack

This incredible miracle, now detailed for the first time,
is the beginning of a work of God that will confirm
His word to Bonnke: *America Shall Be Saved!*

ISBN: (Book) 978-1-60374-952-7 (DVD) 978-1-933446-30-1
SKU: KTEN040
$25.00

Full Flame Film Series

Eight impressive films show how urgent it is for the
Church of Jesus Christ to seek to save the lost. Get rid
of blockages and misconceptions about evangelism.

ISBN: 978-1-933446288   SKU: DVEN019
4 DVD's
$ 50.00

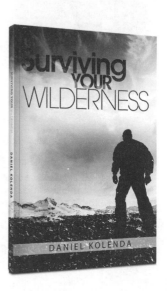